Before They Were President

BEFORE FRANKLIN D. ROOSEVELT WAS PRESIDENT

Gareth Stevens
PUBLISHING

By Michael Rajczak

Please visit our website, www.garethstevens.com. For a free color catalog of all our high-quality books, call toll free 1-800-542-2595 or fax 1-877-542-2596.

Cataloging-in-Publication Data

Names: Rajczak, Michael.
Title: Before Franklin D. Roosevelt was president / Michael Rajczak.
Description: New York : Gareth Stevens Publishing, 2019. | Series: Before they were president | Includes glossary and index.
Identifiers: ISBN 9781538232507 (pbk.) | ISBN 9781538229101 (library bound) | ISBN 9781538232514 (6pack)
Subjects: LCSH: Roosevelt, Franklin D. (Franklin Delano), 1882-1945–Childhood and youth–Juvenile literature. | Roosevelt, Franklin D. (Franklin Delano), 1882-1945–Juvenile literature. | Presidents–United States–Biography–Juvenile literature.
Classification: LCC E807.R35 2019 | DDC 973.917092 B–dc23

First Edition

Published in 2019 by
Gareth Stevens Publishing
111 East 14th Street, Suite 349
New York, NY 10003

Copyright © 2019 Gareth Stevens Publishing

Designer: Laura Bowen
Editor: Therese Shea

Photo credits: Cover, p. 1 (FDR) GraphicaArtis/Archive Photos/Getty Images; cover, p. 1 (ships) Universal History Archive/Universal Images Group/Getty Images; cover, pp. 1-21 (frame) Samran wonglakorn/Shutterstock.com; p. 5 (main) Acroterion/Wikimedia Commons; p. 5 (inset) Mx. Granger/Wikimedia Commons; pp. 7, 11 (main) Historical/Corbis Historical/Getty Images; p. 9 Bachrach/Archive Photos/Getty Images; p. 11 (inset) Tom/Wikimedia Commons; pp. 13, 19 Bettmann/Getty Images; p. 15 MPI/Stringer/Archive Photos/Getty Images; p. 17 (main) Kåre Thor Olsen/Kaare/Wikimedia Commons; p. 17 (inset) FDR Presidential Library & Museum/WFinch/Wikimedia Commons; p. 21 (fireside chat) US National Archives bot/Wikimedia Commons; p. 21 (color portrait) FDR Presidential Library & Museum/Centpacrr/Wikimedia Commons.

All rights reserved. No part of this book may be reproduced in any form without permission in writing from the publisher, except by a reviewer.

Printed in the United States of America

CPSIA compliance information: Batch #CW19GS: For further information contact Gareth Stevens, New York, New York at 1-800-542-2595.

CONTENTS

Franklin's Family Life 4

Education 6

Eleanor 8

Law and Politics 10

World War I 12

Vice Presidential Candidate 14

Living with Polio 16

Governor of New York 18

Road to the Presidency 20

Glossary 22

For More Information 23

Index 24

Words in the glossary appear in **bold** type the first time they are used in the text.

FRANKLIN'S FAMILY LIFE

Future US president Franklin Delano Roosevelt was born January 30, 1882. He was the only child of James and Sara Roosevelt. The wealthy family had a large home near Hyde Park, New York, which was close to the Hudson River. By the time Franklin was 4, he and his father rode horses together around Hyde Park.

During the winter, the family sometimes lived in New York City. In the summer, they traveled to Campobello Island, located off the coast of Maine in New Brunswick, Canada.

Presidential Preview

Franklin's middle name was Delano, which was his mother's last name before she married. People often called him by his **initials**, FDR.

FDR's home was named Springwood, but the Roosevelts usually called it "Hyde Park" or "the Big House." Franklin is pictured here when he was around 2 years old.

YOUNG FRANKLIN

EDUCATION

As a child, Franklin Roosevelt was educated mostly at home. His mother taught him to read. Tutors, or private teachers, taught him German and French as well as other subjects. The family traveled to Europe several times.

When he was 14, Franklin left home to attend school. He went to Groton School, a school for boys in Massachusetts. He played football and baseball but wasn't great at sports. He became a talented member of the **debate** team and sang as well.

Presidential Preview

While at Groton, Franklin helped run a summer camp for poor boys. Groton taught him about the importance of public service.

ROOSEVELT

Franklin was the manager of the baseball team while at Groton.

GROTON BASEBALL TEAM

ELEANOR

Franklin Roosevelt first met his distant cousin Eleanor Roosevelt when he was 4 and she was 2. They saw each other over the years at family gatherings and dances. In 1902, Franklin and Eleanor began to meet up more often, including at a New Year's Eve dinner party at the White House. They grew close.

In 1903, while he was attending Harvard College, Franklin asked Eleanor to marry him. When they married on March 17, 1905, President Theodore Roosevelt, Eleanor's uncle, attended the wedding.

Presidential Preview

During Franklin's time as president, Eleanor often went where FDR couldn't go. He called her his "eyes and ears."

Franklin and Eleanor had six children, though one died as a baby.

ROOSEVELT FAMILY, 1919

LAW AND POLITICS

After Harvard, Franklin Roosevelt went to Columbia Law School. He practiced law in New York City for a short time, but he didn't like it. In 1910, Roosevelt was asked to run for the New York State Senate as a Democrat. Although his **district** had elected Republicans for over 30 years, he ran a strong **campaign** and won the election.

As a state senator, FDR fought to help farmers in his district and worked against **corruption** in government. He learned a lot about **politics** during this time.

Presidential Preview

FDR's respect for his cousin Theodore Roosevelt made him interested in politics. Theodore was president from 1901 to 1909.

FDR, shown here campaigning, was reelected to the New York State Senate in 1912.

PRESIDENT THEODORE ROOSEVELT

WORLD WAR I

In March 1913, President Woodrow Wilson appointed Franklin Roosevelt assistant secretary of the navy, the same position Theodore Roosevelt once held. In 1914, war broke out in Europe. FDR wanted the United States to be prepared to join the war. He called for an increase in the number of sailors as well as new ships.

After Germany attacked American ships, the United States declared war in April 1917 and entered World War I. Under Roosevelt, the navy grew from 197 ships to more than 2,000.

Presidential Preview

During World War I, Roosevelt visited the front lines. He later said, "I have seen war. . . . I hate war." He remembered that as he led the country through World War II (1939–1945) as president.

FDR, then Assistant Secretary of the Navy, pins a Medal of Honor on a naval officer who served during World War I.

VICE PRESIDENTIAL CANDIDATE

The presidential election of 1920 pitted Republican senator Warren G. Harding against Democrat James Cox, governor of Ohio. Cox chose 38-year-old Franklin Roosevelt as his vice presidential running mate. He hoped Roosevelt's famous last name and popularity in New York would help him win the election.

However, the country was still suffering after World War I. Harding promised Americans that, under his leadership, life would return to normal. That promise helped him beat Cox. Even though he lost the election, Franklin Roosevelt had become a nationally known figure.

Presidential Preview

During the campaign of 1920, Roosevelt gave about seven speeches a day.

LIVING WITH POLIO

In 1921, 39-year-old Franklin Roosevelt became ill with poliomyelitis, or polio. This virus usually affects people in childhood. It can harm cells that control muscles, causing **paralysis** and even death. FDR became paralyzed from the waist down.

Roosevelt removed himself from political life. He exercised to overcome his body's limitations. He wore heavy supports called braces on his legs. However, he could walk only short distances, even with the help of **crutches** and canes. He hid his condition from most of the world.

Presidential Preview

In 1924, FDR visited Warm Springs, Georgia. He believed the waters from the springs there helped ease his pain. Roosevelt built a home in Warm Springs that became known as the Little White House.

In 1926, FDR bought Warm Springs and turned it into a world-famous polio treatment center.

ROOSEVELT AT WARM SPRINGS

THE LITTLE WHITE HOUSE

GOVERNOR OF NEW YORK

In 1928, Franklin Roosevelt successfully ran for governor of New York. A year later, the United States entered a time of **economic** troubles called the Great Depression. Many people lost money in the stock market, and banks failed. Few jobs were available.

To help New Yorkers, Roosevelt created jobs and began an unemployment **insurance** plan for those out of work. He also supported providing money for the elderly. After he was elected president, this idea became the Social Security program.

Presidential Preview

When Roosevelt became president, he turned his state programs into **federal** programs. The programs were called the New Deal.

FDR's programs to help people were popular with those struggling during the Great Depression.

ROAD TO THE PRESIDENCY

Republican Herbert Hoover was president when the Great Depression hit the United States. Hoover received some blame for the economic troubles. Many thought his plans to help the suffering nation weren't working fast enough.

FDR knew that many Americans wanted a change. He decided to run for president in 1932. Voters believed in his ideas and elected him. On March 4, 1933, Franklin D. Roosevelt was sworn in as the 32nd president of the United States. He served as president until 1945.

Presidential Preview

After becoming president, FDR gave radio speeches known as fireside chats. They gave Americans hope during the Great Depression and World War II.

Roosevelt's Road to the Presidency

1882	Franklin Delano Roosevelt is born on January 30.
1896	He begins at Groton School, a private school for boys in Massachusetts.
1900	He begins at Harvard College.
1904	He begins at Columbia Law School.
1905	He marries Eleanor Roosevelt on March 17.
1910	He successfully runs for the New York State Senate.
1913	He's appointed assistant secretary of the navy.
1920	He loses the election as a vice presidential candidate.
1921	He becomes ill with polio.
1928	He's elected governor of New York.
1932	Franklin D. Roosevelt is elected the 32nd president of the United States.

FIRESIDE CHAT, 1935

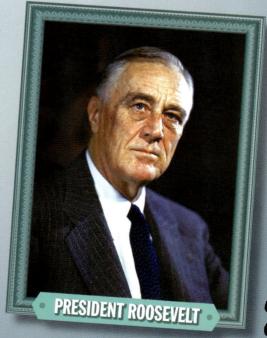

PRESIDENT ROOSEVELT

GLOSSARY

campaign: to take part in a series of activities to support or oppose someone

candidate: a person who is trying to be elected

corruption: dishonest or illegal behavior especially by powerful people

crutch: a long stick with a padded piece at the top that fits under a person's arm

debate: an argument or public discussion

district: an area with a special feature or government

economic: having to do with the economy, or the system by which goods and services are produced, sold, and bought

federal: having to do with the national government

initial: a first letter of a name

insurance: an agreement in which a person makes payments to a company or government in return for money in the event something happens, such as job loss

manager: someone who directs the training and performance of a sports team

paralysis: loss of movement

politics: the activities of the government and government officials

FOR MORE INFORMATION

Books

Brennan, Linda Crotta. *Franklin D. Roosevelt's Presidency.* Minneapolis, MN: Lerner Publications, 2016.

Jurmain, Suzanne Tripp. *Nice Work, Franklin!* New York, NY: Dial Books for Young Readers, 2016.

Krull, Kathleen. *A Boy Named FDR: How Franklin D. Roosevelt Grew Up to Change America.* New York, NY: Dragonfly Books, 2016.

Websites

FDR
www.pbs.org/wgbh/americanexperience/films/fdr/
Visit this PBS website for videos of and about FDR.

Research the Roosevelts
fdrlibrary.org/research-the-roosevelts
Find out more at the presidential library of Franklin Roosevelt.

Publisher's note to educators and parents: Our editors have carefully reviewed these websites to ensure that they are suitable for students. Many websites change frequently, however, and we cannot guarantee that a site's future contents will continue to meet our high standards of quality and educational value. Be advised that students should be closely supervised whenever they access the internet.

INDEX

Columbia Law School 10, 21
Europe 6, 12
fireside chats 20, 21
governor 18, 21
Great Depression 18, 19, 20
Groton School 6, 7, 21
Harvard College 8, 10, 21
Hoover, Herbert 20
Hyde Park 4, 5
Little White House 16, 17
navy, the 12, 13, 21
New Deal, the 18
New York City 4, 10
New York State Senate 10, 11, 21
parents 4, 6
poliomyelitis (polio) 16, 17, 21
presidential election of 1920 14, 15, 21
presidential election of 1932 20
Roosevelt, Eleanor 8, 9, 21
Roosevelt, Theodore 8, 10, 11, 12
Social Security 18
sports 6, 7
Warm Springs 16, 17
Wilson, Woodrow 12
World War I 12, 13, 14
World War II 12, 20